A Christmas Treasury

Volume 2

another collection of joyful holiday readings

from

Our State
NORTH CAROLINA

Greensboro, N.C.

A Christmas Treasury
Volume 2

Published by *Our State* magazine, Greensboro, N.C.

Library of Congress Cataloging-in-Publication Data

A Christmas Treasury, Volume 2 : another collection of joyful holiday readings
from *Our State* magazine.
    p. cm.
 A collection of Christmas stories, quotes, and recipes drawn from the
73-year history of *Our State* magazine.
  ISBN 0-9779681-1-1 (pbk. : alk. paper)
  1. Christmas--Literary collections. 2. American literature--20th century.
3. Christmas--North Carolina--History. 4. North Carolina--Social life and
customs. 5. Christmas cookery. I. *Our State* (Greensboro, N.C.)
  PS509.C56C538 2006
  810.8'0334--dc22
                          2006010600

Contents

Contents

CHAPTER 1

From the Pen of Carl Goerch

No one who met Carl Goerch ever forgot him. A natural storyteller, the editor and founder of The State *magazine was known around North Carolina as an enthusiastic raconteur who combined a no-nonsense outlook with a mischievous sense of humor. Daring enough to start a new weekly publication in the midst of the Great Depression, he offered his original advertisers their money back if, after seeing the first eight issues, they felt it was unworthy of their support. More than 70 years later, his vision lives on in the pages of* Our State.

The Davises

by Carl Goerch

He gave his name as being P. H. Mangum, his residence as being Wake Forest, and he came into my office to renew his subscription to *The State*.

"Well," he said, sitting down for a few minutes' conversation, "it won't be long now before Christmas will be here."

We agreed with him.

He slapped his hand on the desk, broke into a big laugh, and he continued. "I'm 75 years old," he said, "but I'll never forget what happened in the Davis home up near Wake Forest many years ago. I've laughed about it all these years, and I don't believe I'll ever forget it."

He then related the following tale:

George Davis was a farmer and lived about four miles out in the country from Wake Forest. He had three boys — Andrew, who was 8 years old; John, who was 6; and Priestley, who was just about 4. Andrew was a very thrifty sort of boy. He saved his money throughout the year and, a week or so before Christmas, found that he was rich: He actually had 55 cents in cash. It was his own money, and he could spend it on whatever he pleased.

He decided to go to town and buy some Christmas presents for himself. He asked his daddy to let him have one of the mules so he could ride to Wake Forest and back again. Old Man George didn't think much of such extravagance, but he finally gave his consent. So Andrew put a halter on the mule and started for town.

He tied the animal to a hitching post and went into one of the stores. He bought some candy, some nuts, and some fruit. When he asked the storekeeper how much it came to, he was told that it would be 40 cents. He handed over the money.

Just as he was getting ready to leave the store, Andrew saw a big, round, red thing that excited his curiosity, and he asked the storekeeper what it was.

"It's a firecracker," he was told.

"What's that?" Andrew asked.

"You set it off, and it makes a big noise."

"I'll take it," said Andrew.

On Christmas Eve

Andrew put all his purchases in a big paper bag, got up on his mule, and started for home. When he got there, he hid his purchases under the bed where no one would see them. And then, on Christmas Eve, he brought out the bag to show his folks what he had bought for himself.

He spread out the nuts, the fruit, and the candy. Last of all, he pulled out the big firecracker.

"What's that thing?" inquired John, the 6-year-old brother.

"It's a firecracker," said Andrew.

"What does it do?"

"You set it off, and it makes a big noise."

Old Man George was sitting at one end of the room, reading a newspaper. Mrs. Davis was darning socks. They both looked up and gazed curiously at the firecracker.

"How do you set it off?" asked the father.

Andrew hesitated a moment and then admitted, "I don't exactly know."

"Maybe you throw it up against the wall," suggested Andrew. And with that he picked it up and hurled it against one of the walls. Nothing happened. He tried several other experiments without success.

A BIG NOISE, INDEED

Old Man George became impatient. "I told you about wasting your money," he remarked chidingly. "That thing is no-account whatsoever. Next time, maybe you'll have better sense when it comes to spending money that you've had to work hard for."

He then decided that this would be a good time to teach Andrew a lesson. Old Man George got up from his chair, picked up the giant cracker, and hurled it into the fireplace, where a good fire was going at the time. Then, turning his back to the blaze, he shook a finger at Andrew and said, "Don't ever buy anything that — ."

"BOOM!"

There was a terrific explosion. Old Man George fell flat on his face on the floor. Mrs. Davis went over backward in her rocking chair. Live coals scattered all over the floor. Little clouds of smoke began to rise. The two younger boys, scared to death, let out terrific screams.

Old Man George was the first to recover. He saw the live coals and realized that the house was about to burn down. Getting up hurriedly, he ran back into the kitchen, got a bucket of water, and sloshed it vigorously around. He rushed back into the kitchen and got more bucketfuls. Mrs. Davis and the boys were drenched, but the coals finally were put out without any serious damage being done.

Things finally calmed down to some extent, and reasoning faculties returned to Old Man George's mind. His first impression had been that someone had dynamited the house. Now he realized what had happened.

He beckoned to Andrew. "Come on out to the barn with me for a moment," he ordered.

Andrew went reluctantly. The session in the barn was a most painful one but not of long duration. The boys were ordered to go to bed immediately, and that was the end of the excitement.

The next morning when they woke up and went to look into their stockings, Andrew found that the only thing that had been left for him was a switch. He gazed at it ruefully and then, turning to the other two boys, he remarked, "I wonder how Santa Claus found out about that firecracker!"

The State, *December 1951*

Just One Thing After Another

by Carl Goerch

Lots of Northerners are puzzled about the shooting of fireworks down South during the Christmas season. Up North, fireworks are used on the Fourth of July but never on Christmas. Here's how it started:

Back in the good old days, when the population was scattered and communications were difficult, people wanted to wish one another Merry Christmas. The way they did it was for some farmer to get out in his yard and shoot off an old muzzle-loader two or three times. This would be heard and understood by his neighbor, who might be living half a mile away. The neighbor also would start shooting, and the chap who lived on the other side of him would take it up. And that's how this business of fireworks during the Christmas season got started in the South.

When we lived in Washington, North Carolina, folks used to go in quite extensively for Christmas decorations.

Prizes used to be offered for the best decorations.

One Christmas, I had what I thought was a wonderful idea. Getting hold of some loose cotton, I put it in small chunks all over the shrubbery in front of the house. It looked exactly like snow, and the general effect was most impressive.

It was impressive for about three hours. Then a high wind came along and proceeded to blow that cotton all over creation. Some of it went across the Pamlico River and landed in Chocowinity, three miles distant.

We didn't get a prize that year.

We heard the other day about an old bachelor living in Charlotte who has his own way of celebrating Christmas:

The day before Christmas, he wanders along Trade and Tryon streets until he comes across some ragged little urchin, who apparently doesn't have a penny and probably won't have very much of a Christmas.

He takes the kid in tow and leads him into Woolworth's or some other store of that type. Then he tells the youngster to buy anything he likes.

By the time the boy gets through, he is loaded down with toys of every description and is almost crazy with joy. So far as the old man is concerned, it doesn't cost him more than three or four dollars, and it seems to give him the kind of Christmas joy that he wishes to experience.

The State, *December 20, 1947*

Dressing for a Party

by Carl Goerch

The Sphinx Club of Raleigh decided to have a Tacky Party at the Country Club. The idea was for everyone to dress up in old, mismatched, and shabby clothes and look just as tacky as they possibly could.

(Most of the women, when they heard about it, jokingly remarked: "Heavens above! If I just wear my regular clothes I'll look tacky enough." This always brought a laugh, even though the laughter might have sounded just a wee bit forced.)

Anyway, the idea seemed to meet with general approval, so notices of the party were sent out to the various members.

Then, on the morning of the day on which the party was to be held, a hurried meeting of the directors of the club was called. It was revealed at this meeting that only a comparatively small number of members had sent back their cards of acceptance. So small, as a matter of fact, that the directors decided the advisable thing to do would be to call the whole thing off.

A lot of the members were sorry because they already had decided upon all sorts of outlandish costumes to wear.

I had talked it over with my wife and suggested that she wear the dungarees and other garb that she sometimes donned while out in the yard tending to shrubs and flowers.

She sort of demurred but said she might.

When the decision to postpone the event was agreed upon, I suddenly found myself confronted with a terrific temptation. When the idea first came to me, I hurriedly got it out of my mind. But it kept on returning, and with each return, I felt myself getting weaker and weaker.

Complete surrender finally arrived.

When I got home that afternoon my wife said to me, "What time are we supposed to be at the club?" Once more that psychological attribute we call conscience raised its head weakly and protested. All it was able to do, however, was to make a pitifully feeble gesture. Then it subsided completely.

"Oh, about seven o'clock," I told her. "Are you going to wear your dungarees?"

"Do you think it would be all right?"

"Absolutely perfect," I assured her.

"What are you going to wear?"

Uh-oh! I'd forgotten about that. Then an inspiration came to me. "I've borrowed an old golfing outfit from Oscar Davis. I'm going to change clothes at the club — it'll only take a minute."

Nothing else was said at the moment.

AN UNEXPECTED CALL

At six o'clock, the telephone rang. Suddenly I experienced a sort of sinking feeling. I held my breath anxiously and listened carefully.

"I'm sorry, but we're going to the Sphinx Club tacky party. What did you say? Are you sure? Why no — he never said a word about it. Well, I certainly am glad you called me. Good-bye."

She slammed the receiver in its cradle. She entered the living room with fire in her eyes. I risked one hurried glance and then took refuge behind my newspaper.

"Look at me!"

I didn't want to, but I did.

"Did you know that the Sphinx Club party had been canceled?" she demanded.

"Well, er, ah — ."

"Answer me!"

"I believe I did hear something about it this morning," I admitted.

"Why didn't you tell me?"

"I reckon it slipped my mind," I said. "Terribly busy these days, you know. Been working on a special issue of the magazine and we're planning — let me tell you about that."

"I don't want to hear it. Now, you listen to me. You were going to make me go to the Country Club in those dirty dungarees, weren't you?"

"You said you wanted to wear them," I said.

"But I didn't say I wanted to wear them when everybody out there would be dressed in conventional attire," she protested. "How do you suppose I would have looked? What do you suppose people would have thought, with me sitting there, waiting for you to change your clothes?"

The mental picture was too much for me, and I grinned despite everything I could do.

"Oh, yes; it's awfully funny, isn't it?" she asked.

IT REALLY WAS

To tell the truth, it was rather funny, but I hurriedly disclaimed any such idea. "You don't think for a moment that I would have let you gone out in a rig like that, do you?" I asked reproachfully.

"Yes, I do," she said.

"Why, darling — how can you! I was going to wait until you went upstairs to dress, and then I was going to tell you all about it. I've just been kidding you about the whole business. Now, tell me what you want for Christmas."

I tried my best to smooth things over, but I don't believe I made much of an impression. When wives get in the mood that had overwhelmed her at the moment, there's not much you can do or say about it.

I'm afraid, though, that my Christmas present is going to cost me more than I had planned to spend. However, I reckon it'll be more than worth it.

The State, *December 1952*

The Indomitable Mr. Treadwell

by Carl Goerch

This story has to do with Henry R. Treadwell. We don't know Mr. Treadwell. Until Edmund Harding mentioned him to us recently, we had never heard of him.

It seems that he lives in Hagerstown, Maryland, and is associated with the Triangle Grocery Stores. They're a chain of retail stores operating in that part of the country.

Mr. Treadwell is a kindly individual, about 60 years old. He loves people, and he loves to make them happy. For a number of years, he has carried out a little pre-Christmas program in Hagerstown that has proved to be very popular. Here's how it works.

IMPERSONATING SANTA CLAUS

Mr. Treadwell has got a dandy Santa Claus suit. A week or so before Christmas, he dresses up in this suit every evening and proceeds to make a number of visits. He'll go up to the front door of a residence and, when somebody answers his ring, he'll say, "Ho-ho-ho! This is Santa Claus. Does little Tommy Adenoid live here?"

"Yes, he does, Santa Claus," replies Daddy or Mother, as the case may be. Needless to say, they know all about Mr. Treadwell, so they're not at all surprised at seeing him. And then, "Tommy, come out here and see who has called!"

Tommy comes out and stares in wonderment.

"Ho-ho-ho!" says Mr. Treadwell. "So this is little Tommy Adenoid! What do you want old Santa Claus to bring you for Christmas, Tommy?"

Thereupon, Tommy proceeds to reel off a long list of items and Mr. Treadmill (alias Santa Claus) makes a note of them. It's all very exciting, and when Mr. Treadwell finally leaves, Tommy is so excited that he can't go to sleep for a long time.

That same thing takes place many more times during the week before Christmas.

This brings us to Mr. Sanderson — Homer P. Sanderson, vice-president of the Triangle Grocery Stores — who lives about 15 miles from Hagerstown on a big country estate. He had heard about Henry Treadwell's little trick, and he said to him one day, "Henry, I want you to come out to my place this evening and work that little stunt on my two children."

Well, naturally, Mr. Treadwell couldn't refuse the boss's request, so he said he'd be there.

A SUCCESSFUL VISIT

He ate an early supper, dressed in his red suit, put on his whiskers, got into his car, and started for Mr. Sanderson's home. He arrived there safely. His visit was a huge success, and the Sanderson children ate it up. Then Mrs. Sanderson said, "All right, children — to bed, to bed. Santa Claus is going to talk to

Daddy for a little while."

The children went to bed, and the two men talked for quite a while. Then Henry said he reckoned he'd better be starting for home, and he did.

Halfway between the Sanderson place and Hagerstown, Mr. Treadwell's car stopped. He discovered to his horror, amazement, and chagrin that the gasoline tank was empty, and he didn't know where the nearest filling station was.

There was only one thing to do: stop an approaching car and tell the occupants to deliver a message of distress to the first station they came to.

It was an extremely cold night. Mr. Treadwell huddled up on the front seat of the car, anxiously looking up and down the road.

A car showed up, coming from the direction of Hagerstown. As it drew closer, Mr. Treadwell got out and jumped up and down, waving his hands. He was gratified to observe that the car slowed down. It almost came to a stop. Then — S-w-i-s-h!

As it shot past him, Mr. Treadwell thought he detected expressions of fright or surprise on the faces of the driver and the occupant of one of the rear seats.

He got back into the stalled auto again.

In a few minutes, another car. The same thing happened once more. Just as soon as the folks in the car were convinced that they weren't experiencing a hallucination — that they really were seeing Santa Claus, they got away as quickly as possible.

A DISCOURAGING PROCESS

For an hour this continued, and Mr. Treadwell was getting desperate. Another car was approaching. Somewhat slowly, Mr. Treadwell dragged himself out of the car and waved his arms in dispirited fashion. To his great surprise the car stopped. The driver rolled down the window, greeted Mr. Treadwell with a bright smile and said, "Good — hic! — evening, Shannon

Claus. What can I do for you?"

Mr. Treadwell explained his predicament.

The man blinked. "Where's your reindeer?" he inquired. "How come you're riding in an automobile?"

Mr. Treadwell is a quick thinker. He hurriedly explained that he had left his reindeer in Hagerstown so that one of them could be treated by a veterinarian. The man nodded his head, opened the door, and said, "Get in, Shanna Claus and show me where you left them."

Mr. Treadwell directed him to the Treadwell home, got out when they arrived there, and thanked the driver profusely.

"Not at all, Santa Claus. Merry — hic! — Christmas!"

"And a merry Christmas to you!" said Mr. Treadwell.

The State, *December 1952*

CHAPTER 2

Carol Dare Says

*With her ingenious tips and recipes,
The State's own Betty Crocker, Carol
Dare, enlivened December issues
with special holiday flair. Penned by
several columnists over the years,
Dare's words proved that presents
needn't be elaborate or expensive to
express heartfelt Christmas cheer —
and that hospitality is one of the
greatest gifts of all.*

Holiday Tips

Gifts, decorations, and tasty treats

by Carol Dare

A re you ready for Christmas? That's the question friends and neighbors are asking each other every time they meet these days. I do hope you are all through with your Christmas shopping, for there is so little time left to do decorating, cooking, and last-minute wrapping.

SAY IT WITH CANDLES

I've been saving short lengths of candles ever since last Christmas in hopes of making some of my own from them this year.

Someone told me that she made unusual-looking ones by using muffin tins for molds. Melt old candles in a saucepan over low heat, then strain through a sieve into the tins — fancy jelly-type molds make the prettiest finished product. The wick cord may be held in place by inserting the top end in a cardboard round that fits over the mold's top.

A number of these, attractively wrapped, may be the answer to some last-minute gift problems.

One of the most effective front entrance decorations I saw last year were huge red candles, placed on either side of the door, that were made from sections of stovepipe painted with red enamel, then rigged up with lightbulbs attached to electrical cord. You might need the help of someone with special tools to cut tin to fit the top of the pipe and the hole through its center through which to pull the cord.

OLD-FASHIONED 'KISSING HOOP'

For that sprig of mistletoe for a busy doorway, try making an old-fashioned "kissing hoop." Simply wrap two embroidery hoops in red satin, fix one inside the other at a right angle, and tie a cluster of mistletoe in the center. Top with a fuzzy red ribbon bow, and hang where it will surely be put to use.

KIDS' FAVORITE

Bits of bright ribbon left over from wrapping may be made into chain loops and hung from your tree. Do 'em just like you made paper chains in kindergarten days, only you'll find tape much nicer to use than paste.

Tasty decorations

Delight your family by making their favorite congealed salad into miniature Christmas trees. Mold it in pointed, paper water cups. Suspend the cups in small juice glasses while the mixture sets. A red cherry right in the bottom of the cup will be a shiny star of the top of the tree when it is turned out on lettuce.

A good recipe to use for this tree salad is Mrs. B.F. Russell's raw cranberry salad (below), as used in *The Tar Heel Cookbook*, a publication of The Women's Society of Christian Service of Raleigh's Hayes Barton Methodist Church.

1 lb. of cranberries, washed and ground
2 oranges, washed, seeded, and ground
2 cups of sugar

Let set several hours or overnight: 1 box Knox gelatin (four envelopes) mixed with 1 cup cold water.

Add:
2 cups boiling water
2 cups diced celery
2 cups chopped nuts
1 20-ounce can crushed pineapple

Then add the cranberry-orange mixture and let set overnight. Cut into squares for serving. This amount will serve a large crowd; half is enough for an average family.

Irish potato cake

A real old-timey recipe is this one for Irish potato cake. This Southern delicacy, a recipe almost lost to posterity, is still made and served at the Kenlin Hotel in Dodson, which boasts of having housed almost every Superior Court judge in the state, situated, as it is, right next door to the Surry County courthouse.

It is really a fruitcake but without the excess sweetness. In antebellum days it was served with eggnog and toddy.

4 eggs
2 cups sugar
1 cup butter
2 cups flour
1 heaping teaspoon of soda
1 cup of buttermilk
1 cup melted chocolate
1 cup black molasses
1 teaspoon of cinnamon
1 teaspoon of cloves
1 teaspoon of nutmeg
1 teaspoon of lemon juice or flavoring
1 cup walnuts
1 cup seedless raisins
1 cup mashed potatoes

Roll raisins in flour before adding to dough. Follow your regular procedure for mixing butter cakes, and bake in funnel pan in a slow oven.

The State, *December 1953*

Make Merry

by Carol Dare

Take some human nature, as you find it
The commonest variety will do;
Put a little graciousness behind it,
Add a lump of charity, or two.
Squeeze in just a drop of moderation;
Half as much frugality or less,
Add some very fine consideration,
Strain off all poverty's distress,
Pour some milk of human kindness in it,
Put in all the happiness you can.
Stir it up with laughter every minute,
Season with goodwill toward every man,
Set it on fire of heart's affection,
Leave it till the jolly bubbles rise,
Sprinkle it with kisses for confection.
Sweeten with a look from loving eyes.
Flavor it with children's merry chatter,
Frost it with the snow of wintry dells,
Place it on a holly-garnished platter,
Serve it with the song of Christmas bells.

The State, *December 1953*

Holiday Shopping

by Carol Dare

Blessed are they — be they parent, brother, sister, aunt, uncle or grandparent — who are privileged to share Christmas shopping with children. The joy in their hearts, the gleam in their eyes, the excitement in their voices, and the eagerness of their little hands and feet as they go about choosing gifts for friends and loved ones affords enough pleasure to carry the fortunate partner on such an expedition clear through 'til another Christmas.

I know. I've just accompanied my 9-year-old on a one-hour shopping tour of our village. Yes, one hour is all it took; no dillydallying over suitability with her. And yet all her choices were suitable.

A pack of pencils for the college-age sister — 35 cents; squeeze-me toy at 39 cents for her little niece; a package of fancy balloons for the nephew cost a quarter. For their mother, she chose a steel wool chore-girl. She really dug down for that one, marked a whole dollar. But she'd spent a week with this eldest sister the past summer and watched that dish-washing process. Her eyes really sparkle thinking how much help this aid will be.

Friends are easy to buy for; only trouble being that one has a lot of difficulty not playing with such purchases oneself if the wait 'til Christmas is very long. This first shopping spree yielded one dime bank — a dime; one Lone Ranger coloring book — a quarter; a wonderful silvery breast shield — 59 cents. This one is especially tempting.

It was awfully hard making a decision concerning a piece of costume jewelry for Mae-Mae, the beloved maid. But it was more fun than anything else.

"Oh, Mother! Isn't it just beautiful?" she exclaimed as she handled each piece so affectionately. She finally settled on a brilliantly colored brooch for something around 49 cents, plus tax.

We bought a book of stamps for each of the grandmas, though I'll have to admit there was a bit of prompting here. For her daddy, the best of all, she picked the best of all — Cracker Jacks, two boxes. She loves them, too, you see.

There'll need to be one more trip to finish up; there are about a half dozen more folks on her list. Her daddy will be the privileged one next time, for my present must be chosen.

She counted her money last night. There is $2.11 left, not counting her Sunday school money or her silver dollar, which "of course, she would never spend." So I'm making my suggested list. And I need awfully bad:

A new powder puff
Measuring spoons
A sugar scoop
New bridge score pads
Pot holders
Scotch tape
Memorandum pad
Rubber bands
A box of chocolate-covered mints (double checked)

The State, *December 1954*

Jolly Mrs. Nick

by Carol Dare

Jolly Mrs. Nicholas,
Bend your ear this way,
Let's share with our readers,
What we're going to say.
Christmas Eve is coming soon,
Now my dear woman,
How'll I get everything done,
Tell me if you can.

JOHNNY WANTS A PAIR OF SKATES

... and a long list of other things, and he expects me to help treat his room the last day of school. Last year, I worked one whole day and into the night decorating cunning little snowmen cookies. It still makes me tired to think about it.

This year, let Johnny make the treats. Inverted ice cream cones make swell Christmas trees. He can frost them with confectioner's frosting tinted green and decorate with tiny candies.

SUSIE WANTS A DOLLY WITH A GLAMOROUS WARDROBE

I did make a few doll clothes for little Sis, and I really meant to make some for 7-year-old Susie, too, but I'll never get to it.

Do the next best thing: Fit out a sewing box with a lot of interesting materials and trimmings. Include a piece of fur, some imitation pearls from an old necklace, tiny beads, sequins, lace, rickrack, some scraps of velvet and satin, and some tiny artificial flowers. Who knows? Susie may become a famous dress designer some day.

SALLY WANTS A STORYBOOK

A Bible or Bible storybook will make a wonderful gift for 11-year-old Sal. A dictionary or a child's cookbook would be a good choice, too. To make her feel very grown up, give her a magazine subscription.

Sally didn't save enough money to see her through her Christmas gift list, and here at the last minute she wants to make some gifts for her friends and small cousins.

For 50 cents, Sal can purchase a yard of heavy white sailcloth. Give her some snaps and some scraps of felt, and she can make a personal "Happy Holiday Place Mat" for four of her friends. Each fringed mat will be 12 inches by 18 inches. Her imagination and creative abilities will come into play as she cuts motifs from the felt scraps — Christmas trees, valentines, Easter eggs, black cats for Halloween, flags for July 4th, and turkeys for Thanksgiving. Fabric glue will eliminate the need of needle and thread, except for sewing on the snaps. She can arrange it so that her friends can snap the appropriate motif on the lower left hand corner of the mat each holiday.

HUBBY WANTS A PARTY FOR THE OFFICE FORCE

Offer a choice of two beverages. In addition to having one of the old standbys like coffee or eggnog, serve something a little bit different. Try hot, spiced apple juice. Simply simmer juice with whole cloves, stick cinnamon, and a little sugar to taste for about five minutes. Serve a stick of cinnamon in each cup. Or, try other fruit juices — pineapple, apricot nectar, orange-grapefruit, or a combination of these fixed with the spices for a delightful hot punch.

Here's another: Hot Lemonade Punch (from Beth Tartan's Menu Maker and Party Planner). Bring to a rolling boil: 2 cups bottled cranberry juice, 3 1/4 cups water, 1/3 cup sugar, 5 whole cloves, and one stick cinnamon. Cover, remove from heat, and let stand 3 minutes. Strain to remove spices. Pour over thawed concentrated lemonade (one 6-ounce can) and blend. This would be good cold, too.

There are many ways of decorating the table attractively. Probably the easiest is the Christmas package table. Use a white cloth and place wide red ribbon across the table, letting it hang over to the edge of the cloth to look like a package. Place a red ribbon bow where the ribbon crosses and place greenery and shiny ornament or pinecones around the bow.

Another of Beth Tartan's suggestions that appeals to me is the "punch bowl in the snow." Cut a circle of cardboard with a 6-inch margin around the punch bowl. Make a base for the snow by crushing tissue paper around cardboard (with punch bowl in center). Fasten paper to cardboard with straight pins. Then cover paper with soapsuds "snow." This is made by adding a little water to soap flakes and beating with a rotary beater until stiff. While wet, sprinkle "snow" with glitter to catch the candlelight. The snow keeps well and can be done in advance.

As for me, my weary brain isn't very bright; Mrs. Claus, tell Santa to bring me rest and quiet!

The State, *December 1960*

Christmas Cookies

by Carol Dare

Everyone loves Christmas cookies, and here are two simple recipes adapted from *Favorite Recipes of the Lower Cape Fear.*

Christmas Kisses

2 egg whites
1 cup powdered sugar
1 cup chopped nut meats (or 1/2 cup nuts and 1/2 cup coconut)
1 cup chopped dates (or mixed candied fruit)
1 teaspoon lemon, vanilla, or rum flavoring

Beat egg whites until stiff; add sugar and fold in thoroughly. Add remaining ingredients, and drop by spoonfuls on greased cookie sheet and bake at 275 degrees for 20 minutes.

Pecan Rolls

1 3/4 sticks of butter
4 tablespoons powdered sugar
2 cups sifted flour
2 teaspoons vanilla
1 teaspoon water
1 cup chopped pecans

Cream butter with powdered sugar. Add remaining ingredients. Form dough into small rolls, and bake in 275 degree oven. Roll in powdered sugar while still hot.

The State, *December 1960*

Dear Santa

by Carol Dare

I ran across this letter while going through some old
magazines to see what I should keep and what should be
thrown away. This I kept. It struck a responsive chord.
It's from the 1956 December issue of the *Farm Journal.*

Dear Santa,

I want so many things to help me be a good mother to
our four.

Could you bring me a calm voice to replace my frenzied
one? I could do with a supply of patience, too. My stock was
rather small to begin with, and it has dwindled alarmingly
what with teenage phone calls, daily battles over homework,
and the pet turtle getting loose.

What do you have that would help me keep order among
our family's unfiled clippings and articles? Every family needs
handy information on dinosaurs, atomic research, and the
culture of ancient Rome — but my husband looks at me

strangely when he opens a closet door and a box of clippings falls on his head. (Maybe you could bring him a crash helmet.)

I also need a Handi-Dandy Mind Reader's Magic Menu and Meal Maker guaranteed to put a stop to cries like, "But we already had that spaghetti glop at school."

And Santa, darling, if you have any leftover hours, please drop them down our chimney. It would be wonderful to have some time every day for thinking deep thoughts, reading Shakespeare, and prettying up myself.

Now, in case you think I don't want to give as well as receive, I'd like you to know that I'll gladly give you 30 or 40 nice chubby pounds I've managed to pick up along the way.

Merry Christmas!

The State, *December 1958*

CHAPTER 3

Readers Remember

The Christmas season evokes memories unique to every North Carolinian. Some fondly recall the warmth of a Yule log or a charitable act while others treasure their youthful days of hand-picked trees and homemade cakes.

Whatever the circumstances, it's clear that the best memories have one thing in common — the love and comfort that accompanies the presence of family and friends.

The Christmas Log

by John A. Parris

Aunt Ede's grandson, Nelse, rode up in his wagon just at dusk with a big water-soaked hickory stump. Grandpa Parris used to say there was nothing like a water-soaked hickory stump for a Yule log. Grandpa knew, for he was a mountain man. When he was a boy, it was his job to fetch the Yule log, and later, when he had sons, it was their job to search out the hickory stumps on Little Savannah.

By the time I came along, we were living in town. Our fireplace had a grate, and we couldn't have a hickory stump. But Dad always took me to Grandpa's during Christmas, and there was the big hickory stump blazing and simmering in the big fireplace where Grandma did a lot of her cooking.

Looking at the stump Nelse had fetched down from the mountain, I thought that somehow it didn't look as big as the stumps remembered at Grandpa's as a little boy.

I said, "Nelse, you sure this is the biggest hickory stump you could find?" He looked at me and then at the stump.

"Why, that stump'll burn for a month of Sundays. It'll be all right. I reckon my grandmammy would've been proud to see such stump as that. I've heard my mammy say back in olden times when her mammy was a slave that it was the custom for everybody to just rest and fold their hands long's the Yule log burned. The white folks lit it on Christmas Eve, and, sometimes, my mammy said her mammy said that ol' Yule log'd burn for two whole days, maybe three. Times shore have changed, and that's a true fact."

Yes, times have changed, I said, thinking on the size of Grandpa's logs and sitting around his hearth on Christmas day listening to him tell about the Christmas he was snowed in and the other Christmases, some that sounded like fun and others that sounded pretty grim, even to a 10-year-old boy.

"Reckon I'll be gettin' on toward home," said Nelse. "It looks like it's fixin' to weather-up."

While we had stood there, flurries of snow had started blowing down from the peaks that towered dark above the valley.

"If this keeps up," said Nelse, "I reckon we will have us a shore 'nough white Christmas. My ol' bones start achin' when it snows."

I watched Nelse climb up into the wagon and ride off. The clop-clop-clop of the mule and the squeak of wheels were only a whisper from down the road when finally I picked up a couple of logs from the stack beside the door and moved on inside to mend the fire.

In the past few minutes, darkness had come on with a suddenness, and the only light in the paneled room was that from the big fireplace. I tossed the logs on the fire, then sank down into a chair. Sitting there I watched the flames dance along the logs of birch.

The birch tossed flames to which you could attach a face,

a figure, even a voice. And suddenly the flames etched into life a scene from out of the long ago . . .

It was a snowy Christmas, and Grandpa was 87. Mother and Dad and I had driven the eight miles out from town and parked the Model T under the apple tree across the creek from Grandpa's. We carried presents for Grandpa and Grandma, who lived all alone since their sons had grown up and moved into town.

Standing by the Model T while Mother heaped my arms with packages, I looked over toward the house, which wore a shawl of snow, and, watching the blue wood smoke curl up from the chimney, I asked Mother if she thought Grandma would bake me some johnnycake on the hearth. Mother said she guessed she might if I was real nice about it.

When we got to the house, we found Grandpa sitting by the fire, all hunkered over the flames, and he said he couldn't seem to get warm. "Been havin' chills all day," he said.

Even before I took off my coat I went over to him and handed him a little package all done up in red paper and tied with a piece of green ribbon. He took the package and laid it down beside his chair, but I said he was supposed to open it right then. He reached down and got it and opened it and smiled at me as he held up the pocketknife I had picked out all by myself. He gave it to Grandma and told her to lay it on the mantel.

For a moment he just sat there staring into the fire and was all quiet, not like he usually was when I came to see him. Then he pulled me to him like he always did and hugged me, and a little later he reached into his pocket and took out a bright, shiny silver dollar.

"I've been so poorly, son," he said. "I couldn't get into town to get you anything for Christmas. This is the best I can do."

And then he took my hand and put a silver dollar in it

and closed my fingers around it. I thought it was the finest present I had ever had. I knew right then I never would spend it.

Grandma said she was about to fix supper, but Mother said the weather was so bad we would have to get back before dark. Grandma asked if we wanted to spend the night, but Mother shook her head and said Santa Claus wouldn't know where I was, and Grandma smiled and ran her hand through my hair.

Then Grandma offered me some johnnycake and sweet milk, knowing how much I loved it, and I looked at Mother, and she nodded and I asked, "Would you bake it on the hoe like you sometimes do, Grandma?" And she said, "Why, bless you, honey, I will."

While Grandma was gone back to the kitchen to mix up the batter, Grandpa said this was the first time since he and Grandma had been married that they hadn't had a Yule log.

"It don't seem like Christmas," he said, and Dad nodded his head but didn't say anything.

Mother looked at Dad, but he wasn't looking at her; he was staring into the fire.

And Grandpa said, "I'm not as young as I used to be, and I've got no one to go out and fetch me a hickory stump." He paused and looked at Dad, then went on, "Boy, remember them big hickory stumps you used to drag in?" And Dad nodded again, still not saying anything.

Then Grandpa was quiet, and he reached down and picked up a little bitty hickory log and tossed it on the fire.

Finally, Dad said, "Pa, has the mule been fed?" And Grandpa looked at him and said, "I reckon. Jim Pott's boy has been lookin' after him for me, though he's not been by the house yet."

"Think I'll have a look," Dad said. I said I would go with him, but he shook his head and went on back through the house toward the back door and the path that led out across the branch to the barn.

"Now why do you suppose he got interested all of a sudden in that mule?" said Grandpa.

Mother shook her head.

About that time Grandma came back. She had a bowl of batter in one hand and a hoe in the other.

Grandma said, "Where's John?" And Grandpa told her that he went to see about the mule.

Then Grandma bent down and dipped her hand into the batter and spread some of it on the hoe blade. With the edge of the hoe turned toward the fire she leaned the handle against the top of the fireplace. The batter started steaming and simmering and turning gold-like.

Grandma went back to the kitchen to fetch me a glass of sweet milk, and when she came back the johnnycake was all brown. She handed me the milk, then bent down and broke off a hunk of the johnnycake for me. It was almost too hot to eat. I would take a bite of it and then a swallow of the milk to cool it off.

While I ate, Mother and Grandpa and Grandma talked about this and that, stuff that didn't interest me. Once Mother said she wondered what was keeping Dad, and then they talked about Grandma's other sons and their children, and, by that time, I had stuffed down all of the first johnnycake, and Grandma had cooked me another one.

It was beginning to get dark, and Dad had been gone over most of an hour. Mother said that she was a little concerned. Grandpa said maybe he was talking to Jim Pott's boy and had plumb forgot the time. Mother said if he didn't come soon we would never get home. Then they went back to talking about something else.

Grandpa's clock on the mantel struck five, and Mother said she was going out to see what had happened to Dad, but just then we heard a clomping and a stomping on the porch. The door opened, and there was Dad, all covered with snow from head to feet.

Mother took one look at him and said, "Where've you been?" and Dad sort of grinned and shook the snow from his shoulders.

"Doing something that I used to do," said Dad, grinning again.

He told me to hold the door open for him, and then he went back outside. Grandma came to the door and said, "Land sakes!" and Grandpa said, "What is it?" Mother started to get up, but by that time Dad was backing through the door saying, "Easy does it."

Dad had ahold of one end of a big log, and Jim Pott's boy had ahold of the other end. They toted it right into the room and right up to the fireplace, and then they eased it down into the fire where the other logs had just about burned out.

"There's your hickory stump," said Dad, looking at Grandpa. "Now don't say you haven't got a Yule log. Of course, it's not like the ones I used to fetch when I was a boy, but I didn't have much time to look around in this snow."

Grandpa seemed to perk up for the first time, and he smiled at Dad, then lowered his head and got out his handkerchief and blew his nose. "Reckon that hickory stump'll heat up this place and cure my cold," he said.

Dad gave Jim Pott's boy a dollar and told him to see that the mule was put up in the barn, and then we were all laughing and talking at once and watching the hickory stump begin to catch fire.

Mother said we'd better be going, and Dad said he guessed so. She got up and helped me into my coat. Dad held open the door for us, and it was dark as we said "Merry Christmas" to Grandpa and Grandma.

Both of them had come to the door, and both of them were smiling — Grandpa said he already felt better. Then we were out in the night, tramping through the snow to the Model T.

Dad cranked up the Model T and got in, and Mother said to him, "You probably got your death of cold," but her voice wasn't sharp. There was something proud in it. She reached across me and touched Dad's arm and then looked back toward the house where Grandpa and Grandma sat before the fire that now was eating into the hickory stump Dad had fetched, like he had when he was a boy.

It had stopped snowing as Dad backed the Model T out into the road and headed her for home. ...

The scene faded from the flames of my own fire as Dorothy came into the room and said, "Asleep?" I laughed and said, "Just dreaming."

"We'd better have some light," she said, and I agreed.

But before I got up and walked over to the wall switch, I said, "Nelse brought our Yule log, but it doesn't look as big as the ones Grandpa used to have."

And then I felt in my pocket, and my fingers caressed a silver dollar.

The State, *December 1955*

Christmas at the Cherokee Mission

by Connaree K. Highfill

E ach year we had a balsam Christmas tree that reached to the
ceiling placed in a corner in Sequoyah Hall. George Owl was
in charge of decorating the tree and the hall, and the total
scene presented a beautiful sight. Huge logs were piled in the broad
and deep rock fireplace. The glow of the blazing fire added both
warmth and color to the happy Christmas party. Rows of chairs for
adults were placed in a semi-circle facing the Christmas tree. Small
chairs were placed in front for the little ones. Under and around the
tree the gifts were piled high.

Friends of the Cherokee Mission from far and near sent and
brought carloads of presents. Not only did the Cherokee
members and their families receive gifts, but also those "pale faces"
that worked with them, for that was the way that the Cherokee
wanted it.

One year there were many toys left over to be stored for the
following year. But wait: Down the road was a family with little

children whose parents had no winter jobs. So my little helper, Glenn Tolley, and I piled our arms high with story books, puzzles, toy trucks, dolls, and treats and away we went. It didn't take long for the boys in that home to get down on the floor with their trucks and toys or for the little girls to hold the dolls close.

Meanwhile, the church bus was making its first run up Soco Road and later up Bigwitch Mountain, while the station wagon was going to Birdtown and out the Mission Road to bring the people to the Center. As the chimes were pealing out "Hark, the Herald Angels Sing," Glenn and I felt that the angels were singing for us also as we tripped back to Sequoyah Hall.

Soon the people were gathered in, and Mrs. Anita Larch read the Christmas Story from Luke's Gospel. She did it so touchingly, so beautifully.

You see, Anita did not speak one word of English when she entered the Cherokee boarding school many years before. At home she had spoken only her native Cherokee language. She appreciated being able to read her Bible in both the Cherokee and English languages. After her graduation from the Carlisle Indian School she had taught in the Cherokee schools.

After singing many of the Christmas carols, we closed the worship service with the singing of that most beloved song of Christmas, "Silent Night, Holy Night."

Then old Santa came in and, with his helpers, gave out the gifts and treats to all. There were happy faces, shining eyes, and children's laughter, as shouts of "Merry Christmas" were heard amid the rattling of toys, blowing of horns, and beating of drums.

As our Cherokee friends returned to their homes on the mountains, each family was carrying a new flashlight to light their way up the well-beaten trails. There was an afterglow of love, peace, and joy in our hearts, for those lights had come on in a greater way for a noble people in the Great Smoky Mountains of western North Carolina.

The State, *December 1979*

The Stable

by Eunice Pitchford

As a little boy, Charles thought our nativity figures belonged in a stable. But we didn't have a stable. He brought out his Lincoln Log set and constructed one, put a piece of cardboard across the top for a roof, and covered it with moss. Inside he placed the figures representing the Holy Family, the angel on the rooftop, and the wise men and shepherds enroute. The only problem with Charles's stable was that if anybody accidentally bumped it, he had to rebuild.

The years went by, and the little boy was big enough to take his daddy's tools and turn creative. He found lumber scraps and busily hammered and sawed and nailed, making a box-like shelter that wouldn't fall down if bumped. He disguised it with the usual moss covering and arranged the scene as he felt proper.

The rest of the family did the other decorating, but he was the official family member in charge of the nativity scene, for he had built the stable.

The years rolled on, and Charles was college age. He and a friend next door decided store-bought Christmas trees were already dying before hitting the market and that we should have a freshly cut tree. Annual pilgrimages were made into woods, and the trees brought into our house got so big we had to move the dining room table into the living room and set up the pine in the very middle of the dining room floor. The electric train, long stored away, was brought out, and one Christmas Eve he sanded track until 2 a.m. so all would function perfectly. But the same little stable was carefully set out, mossed over, and the figures were put into proper places.

Charles is now married and in a home of his own. His ideas of Christmas decor have changed little. I was once there when he brought in his carefully selected and freshly cut tree — and he is still looking for just the right nativity set and will make a stable to use in establishing his own home's Christmas tradition.

The State, *December 1981*

Mama's Cakes

by Mildred Southerland Suitt

Sometimes I hear folks talking about the cakes their Mothers used to make, and I get to thinking about the ones Mama made, especially those she made for friends and neighbors whose hearts were aching. She called these "Comfort Cakes," and one day she told me about the unwritten message she put into them.

Any time Mama made a cake was a wonderful time, but Christmas was best of all. You had such a variety to choose from that it was mighty hard to decide just which kind you wanted put on your plate.

Do you remember old-fashioned jelly cake? It was made with yellow layers, put together with a tart jelly, and sometimes topped with a fluffy white seven-minute frosting. It was so yummy!

Devil's food cake was made with dark chocolate layers, and you had a choice of fillings — seafoam, made with light brown sugar or white sugar, or chocolate fudge filling.

Spice cake was so good — it made the house smell real

Christmasy.

Lady Baltimore cake was my sister Lillian's favorite. This was made with yellow layers. The filling was a rich ground-up mixture of raisins and walnut meats, and the cake was then crowned with a soft white frosting. Perfect, large walnut halves and raisins were used to make pretty designs. (Mama's decorating always gave you the real clue to the goodness inside.)

Old-timey lemon cake, made with yellow layers and a gooey lemon filling, was Grandmama Southerland's choice.

Caramel cakes were yellow layers with a rich filling made with brown sugar and were a favorite at our house.

Fruit cake was made especially for holiday-time and was so filled with goodies that we called it the "Goody Cake."

Daddy's favorite was a fluffy coconut cake, which looked like a large snowball and was almost too pretty to cut. The coconut cakes were never decorated. They were so perfect they didn't need it. Mama said it would be like tying a bow of ribbon on an American beauty rose!

Strawberry shortcake and banana shortcake were so delicious you ate them slowly to make the luscious goodness last a long time.

Remember how you had to tiptoe around the house while pound cake was baking? Half the joy of this cake was in the delicious aroma, and half was in the eating.

Angel food cake always made Daddy laugh. He called it "air cake" or a "bunch of nothing."

I like to think about the large sheets of plain yellow cake that Mama made. These were cut into squares and eaten with homemade banana ice cream in the summer time.

I used to look forward to the days we had molasses cake, which was made in a large pan and cut into squares. On these days, Mama would make a batch of small molasses cakes for afterschool snacks.

Each of these cakes I will always remember, but the one that stands out in my memory is the "Comfort Cake," which had an unwritten message from Mama. Beneath the dark swirls of chocolate frosting — the sorrow your troubled heart was experiencing — you found the sunshine in her golden layers. The message was as clear as if Mama had written it in her beautiful handwriting.

The State, *December 1979*

The Traditional Cedar

by Carl Cahill

When I was a child, our Christmas trees came from the woods and fields around Spencer, the little North Carolina town where I was born.

Each year my father and I hiked into the countryside, usually to the west of Grant's Creek, until we found a symmetrical red cedar. He would fell the tree and carry it home, sometimes a mile or two away, and stand it on X-shaped boards nailed to the butt. Then we would decorate it with paper chains my sister and I had pasted together in elementary school.

There were no Christmas trees for sale in Spencer during the Depression. Like us, other residents selected their trees from nearby farms, whose owners never objected. Trespassing was a little-known word. There were plenty of cedars, and we were careful to close gates so the cows wouldn't wander free. The use of other evergreens for Christmas trees was also unknown to us. If it wasn't a cedar, it wasn't a Christmas tree. A cedar tree stayed green for weeks after it was cut, even without water, and it filled the house with a fragrance I still associate with gifts and good things to eat.

Now, four and a half decades later, the sale of scotch pines, blue spruce, and fir is a multi-million dollar business. But nowhere can a cedar tree be found on a commercial lot. Now, too, "No Trespassing" signs abound.

Still, traditions are meant to be kept, and each year, like my father, I take an ax and go into the fields and woods around the little Virginia community where we now live, cut down a red cedar, and bring it home, sometimes laboring under its weight for a mile or more.

Young guests at our house look at it and exclaim, "A cedar tree! I've never seen a cedar Christmas tree before." Older guests are startled to recall suddenly that when they were children they had cedar trees in their homes at Christmas.

But the tradition is getting harder to keep. Homes cover much of the countryside. "Keep Out" notices are difficult to avoid, and more and more time is needed to scout out the few well-shaped, proper-size trees remaining.

So this year, on Thanksgiving morn, while the rest of the family prepared the afternoon feast, my youngest child and I set out — this time by canoe — to a remote, uninhabited place to look for a cedar Christmas tree.

We found three — perfectly shaped, deep green, and so full my hand hardly could penetrate to the trunks. I tied strips of white cloth to them as markers.

A week before Christmas we will return and narrow the choice to one, load it into the canoe, and paddle home.

This annual excursion into the woods for a cedar Christmas tree means little to anyone except myself. I've never told my family of its importance to me.

But Christmas is the time for traditions, and I shall keep this one as long as I can.

The State, *December 1981*

The Wagon Ride

by Linda S. Chandler

My fondest and most thrilling memory of the years when I visited my grandparents' farm in Anson County concerns a trip by wagon at night to a church for a Christmas program.

I was very young — about 5 years old. My parents were still young and my grandparents middle aged and exuberant. The boys, my uncles, were teenage and full of zing. They were such a happy family unit, and on this particular evening they had loaded a farm wagon with hay, hitched up two mules, thrown about a dozen quilts in for cover, and we all got in and started down the country road to church.

We stopped along the way at neighbors' houses to pick up more passengers, and when the wagon was filled, we rolled steadily through the night. The dirt road was frozen hard; the wheels hitting the ruts and rocks made a bumping, jarring, uneven ride, but we didn't mind. The singing! The laughing! The snug excitement as I was sandwiched in between the adults under the quilts on the scratchy warm hay. My mind does not furnish any details concerning the service, the return trip home, or any other activity. I must have fallen asleep.

All these years I have remembered the crisp, cold December night and the bright stars above us. I recall so fondly the spirit of happy excitement. If I had to go back in time to an event of special pleasure and significance, it would be that Christmas season activity.

The State, *December 1979*

CHAPTER 4

In Finest Tradition

Special poems, a unique Christmas card from Annie Oakley, a popular ballad by John Jacob Niles, and a majestic giant holly tree in Pamlico County all have roots among the Old North State's greatest holiday rituals.

Snapshots of
Christmas Memories

by Bill Sharpe in 'Thursday'

Christmas-tree-cutting parties, spreading out into the nearby woods to get trees. It was considered cricket to ask the landowner for permission to cut down the cedar, but it was not always done. Only the older boys ventured after mistletoe — that involved climbing formidable trees. No one thought about buying such things, and, in fact, no one thought about selling them. Saving for Christmas started after the Fair — it could not possibly start before then.

The groups of Christmas caroling children. Sunday School Christmas "entertainments" with my uncle — a Santa Claus chosen solely for corpulency — coming out of a cardboard chimney to distribute hard candy and oranges to the children. The thousands of children who always wanted a pony and cart and, of course, never got one. The kids who sat on their front porches on a warm, sunny Christmas, with a bright new sled beside them, forlornly praying for snow.

Country cousins

Our cousins in the country did not hang up stockings but left shoeboxes out, with their names scrawled thereon. Next morning the boxes were found full of such exotic things as coconuts, raisins, bananas, oranges. On the table was a wooden tub of stick candy — enough to make everyone sick.

A homemade Christmas confection was to take a piece of lemon stick candy, ream it with a hot hairpin, and use it as a straw to suck juice out of the oranges, but I have not seen that done in 25 years. An enormous country Christmas dinner, featuring turkey, fried rabbit, and four kinds of cake, including "checkerboard chocolate" made with an ingenious pan which alternated chocolate and white filling. But first, a Christmas morning rabbit hunt by the big boys, proudly toting double-barreled shotguns bought with their own tobacco money. It seemed very strange, but Santa Claus did not bring presents to the country — only goodies and clothes.

Snow on Christmas Day

There was that miraculous snowy Christmas morning and being awakened in the yet dark to hear my father singing "See the pretty snow come down; Earth is putting on a royal crown; royal, royal, royal crown! Earth is putting on a royal crown!" which we knew was reserved only for snowy singing. Christmas and snow on the same day — it was too much.

Getting ready for Christmas meant making wreaths on a frame of stove wire but especially making tree trimmings that were on the Sunday School tree ... At home, corn was popped and strung in long white ropes — with, of course, enough corn popped for eating purposes at the same time. Everyone could make "chains" of colored paper, looped and pasted with flour paste. Then cardboard stars were cut out of shoeboxes and carefully covered with tinfoil recovered from cigarette boxes.

Typical Christmas presents: red galluses with gold snaps, B.B.

air-rifles, homemade peanut brittle, games like jack-straws, flinch, and checkers. And oh, those out-of-season presents, like tops, pee-tads, and baseball mitts; they were given because it was at Christmas or never. Of course, no Christmas was complete without a jack-knife, which, however, rarely survived to barefoot time. In a world of bows and arrows, reed-whistles, "wawkin sticks," gourd dippers, and general random whittling, a boy was out of luck without some sort of knife.

Something from the kitchen

The few days before Christmas also largely concerned the grocery store and the kitchen. Scents which alternately weakened youngsters and then aroused in them their thieving instincts arose from the kitchen. Great lard-cans full of crisp cookies were stored against the coming holiday, lavish cakes (including three huge fruit cakes) went into the "safe" as did walnut-studded fudge, red and green mints, and sometimes a confection called "sea-foam." Christmas was one time when my mother, ordinarily prudent, refused to scrimp on her cooking.

Or so I remember it.

The State, *December 1972*

Greetings from
'Little Sure Shot'

by Ashton Chapman

D id Annie Oakley send the first personalized, printed
Christmas card ever mailed? Her biographer, Walter
Havighurst, says she did. She created the design and
sent out her own "personal" cards for the Christmas of 1891
and for many Christmases thereafter.

It is sure that these included the years when she and her
husband, Frank Butler, were on the staff of the Carolina Hotel
at Pinehurst, for which a Tar Heel friend bears witness.

Annie always made friends readily. Those she made at
Pinehurst included such celebrities as John D. Rockefeller Sr.,
John Philip Sousa, Walter Hines Page, Booth Tarkington, and
Edgar A. Guest. They also included a small Pinehurst girl who
never forgot her.

In 1959, Mrs. G.H. McCormick of Monroe wrote me about
her association with Annie: "She was a personal friend of mine
when I was just a little girl living in Pinehurst, and I always

received a Christmas card on which her picture appeared, wishing me a Merry Christmas. I have no idea where any of them are except the one that for some reason I saved. The picture depicts her as Sitting Bull in 1919 at the annual masked ball at Hotel Wentworth, and for which she won first prize."

THE VERY FIRST

Creation of the first Christmas card is generally credited to the English painter J.C. Horsley, R.A., who drew a design for one in 1843. As late as the beginning of the Gay Nineties, so few printed designs were available that persons would receive from their friends numerous duplicates of the Christmas cards they themselves had sent out. The only difference often lay in the engraved visiting cards that were delivered with them.

Before 1900, few cards were signed or mailed. Usually they were delivered by hand, accompanied by the sender's formal visiting card.

SPECIAL GREETINGS

Annie Oakley's now-famous Christmas card of 1891 was a folder with her picture on the cover. She was wearing a Western-type hat and her numerous marksmanship medals. Framed in sprays of cattails and their long, slender foliage were the words "Little Sure Shot," the name by which she was affectionately know far and wide, printed beneath the picture.

Inside were two scenes. One, with the caption "Christmas in the West," showed a log cabin amid snowy woods with a slender girl (presumably Annie herself) waving to a sleigh-load of arriving visitors. The other picture of a mansion on New York's Fifth Avenue was captioned "Christmas in the East."

On the back cover were an "O.A." monogram and "Annie Oakley's Christmas Greeting" above this original verse:

"I've built me a bridge of kindest thoughts
Over the ocean so wide;
And all good wishes keep rushing across
From this to the other side."

Havighurst says that Annie planned the card herself, made a sketch of it, wrote the lines, then took them, in November 1891, to a printer in Glasgow, Scotland. This was during the first winter of the triumphal European tour of Buffalo Bill's Wild West Show, of which Annie was such an important attraction.

To emphasize her message on the back cover, Annie instructed the printer to show in the margin a string of seagulls flying, with her Yuletide greetings, across the water.

Of the hundreds of these cards, which found their way across the Atlantic to fully half the states in the Union, few have been preserved. One is known to be in a private collection in New York. Another is on exhibit in the Darke County Museum, near Annie's birthplace in Ohio.

Annie was past 50 when she and her husband accepted the offer to join the Pinehurst staff for their first of four successive winters at the popular Sandhills resort. She was white-haired and "thin as a reed," but her skill as a marksman was undiminished.

The State, *December 1967*

Twelfthnighters

by W.C. Burton in The Greensboro News

Holley Mack Bell, a nimble editorial brain on this journal and an amiable and scholarly friend, has just been elected permanent president of the World Wide Association of Twelfthnighters.

The credo, rules, and bylaws of the Twelfthnighters are all as simple as day — or as simple as the Twelve Days — and are rolled into one grand plan. We believe in observing the full Christmas season. We point out — to all who will hear — that the Christmas season begins on Christmas Eve and continues until Epiphany, sometimes called Old Christmas, January 6.

In this way the true celebrant gets a sort of bonus of two extra days since this runs to 14 days, but that's all right. The 12-day count begins, of course, on the day after Christmas Day — when the wise men saw the star.

If I understand anything at all about the Christian spirit, as I conceive it to be in its true form, then Christmas best expresses it. Christmas, with all of its color and gaiety, warmth and affection, charity and jollity, tinsel, Christmas trees, and Santa Claus — all these are a part of a truly good way. This, I feel, should be the complexion of the Christian spirit all the year 'round. The holiday trappings, wonderful in their proper place, are not necessary to the general practices of the spirit.

Twelve Months

For this good and sufficient reason, the Twelve Days of Christmas are also symbolic of the 12 months of the year in my mind.

It should be made clear that neither Holley Mack nor I nor any true Twelfthnighter endorses — or even contemplates — the continuation of the frantic and strenuous aspects of Christmas for a dozen added days. Far from it. Indeed just the opposite is true. We advocate the Twelve Days as a relaxed time, a stay-at-home time, or quietly-visit-your-friends time. It may contain parties if you like parties, or none if you like none.

Above all, it is time to think and feel and savor and soak up Christmas. It is a season for good books, good talks, good recollections, and quiet happiness. It is a family time and a time for all men, women, and children. It is a time for deep and sweet awareness.

To some it may seem that the program of the Twelfthnighters is a little limited, devoted wholly to a relatively short period of the year. It's true that our prime aim is the full enjoyment and observance of Christmas. I should like to say at this time, however, that we carry on a highly attractive year-long program in an unobtrusive way.

An Invitation

We also encourage celebration of Easter, St. Valentine's Day, the Fourth of July, Labor Day, Thanksgiving Day,

St. Swithin's Day, Groundhog Day, and the vernal equinox. We advocate candlelight and wine, firelight and friends, and moonlight and romance if circumstances permit. We have come out unequivocally for fresh snowfall, spring showers, autumn dusks, and summer nights. We place our seal of approval on a wide variety of articles and institutions including good pictures, good reading, sweet repose, the laughter of children, sunsets, Bertie County ham, pretty girls, democracy, the sanctity of the home, turtle watching, and time-and-a-half for overtime.

Won't you join us?

The State, *December 1960*

A Christmas Poem

by W.C. Burton

Mr. Burton writes a column in the *Greensboro Daily News* titled "Professor Burton's Class." In 1962, this poem appeared there, and we thought you would enjoy it as much as we did.

When skies in winternight
Are darkly crystal clear,
And stars are piercing bright
And steely blue and near,
I do not need a calendar
With eleven pages torn away,
The fragments of eleven paper months,
Three and two-thirds imprinted seasons,
Impinged by steel staples, reminders
That they were there, are gone,
Are done and spent (Where did the summer go?
And the spring? And the fall?);
Nor any other man-made marker

Do I need to tell me, surely,
Christmas is coming,
Is almost here,
Is here!!!
I do not need the days of weeks
Or months checked off,
Or the dates on newspapers
Or on magazines, bright
With colored ink, making
Familiar images and symbols,
Images of wreathes and candles,
And green cones of trees
In gems of glass and foil
And silver garlands,
And Santa Claus
With cherub smile
And rosy nose
And silken, hoary whiskers,
And cheery firesides (stocking-hung)
Coziness and comfort,
Or pictures of people smiling
And holding new things,
Shiny and just broken
Out of the shimmering, sumptuous,
Tissue and metallic eggshell
Of fancy gift-wrapping.
No indeed.
When daylight's shining sun
Is briskly, sweetly clean
And softest clouds are spun
In vaulted blue serene,
I do not wait for windows
To tell me the season
Or the season's secrets

Or the season's delights,
With lights and ornaments
Reflecting gaiety and cheer
(Albeit some commerce, too.)
Is filled with pearly glow,
And mystery tints the gray
As vapors shift and flow
I search out no records
Or calibrations,
Or works of reference,
Or rules or guides
Or almanacs,
That I may say firmly
"Yes, it's the Yuletide."
No pictures, ikons, artifacts
Must stand to announce
This time, this place
In the moving year
Of men and angels,
This gentlest and jolliest
Of seasons all,
This treasured, blessed
Christmas time.
The surest signs are in the sky
And in the earth, and the waves
Of known, yet unknown energy,
That flash between all men
Who are of good will
Or who seek good heart.
Oh, I can not explain it.
I can only say that it is something –
The texture, tempo, feel of things,
Some way the dusk may fall, the morning break,
Some way a thing may echo in the mind

And in the heart.
Or some reverberation in the air,
Some distant sound, a bell —
Not rung by hands of man
And certainly not machine —
The heartbeat of a child
Or of just a young heart,
Whatever age its cage of ribs.
Maybe it is many hearts
Beating time to joy
I do not know.
I only know
I know the time.
I see and feel
The Christmas time!

The State, *December 1965*

Birth of a Ballad

by Nancy Alexander in Lenoir News-Topic

Did you know one of the loveliest of all Christmas carols was found in North Carolina hills? John Jacob Niles, well-known folklorist, was roaming the hills of the state in the 1930s recording ballads when he chanced to hear an appealing tune.

Niles was strolling along the streets of Murphy when he heard a small voice in a crowd singing a plaintive tune in a minor key. Pushing through the people on the street, he stopped a little girl who'd been singing and asked her to repeat the song.

Niles realized as she sang and he recorded the lyrics of "I wonder as I wander out under the sky..." that he was hearing something very old and rare. He questioned the pathetic child about the song. She replied simply that she'd known it always. She didn't remember where she'd learned it or who had taught it to her.

Niles found the child's name was Annie Morgan. A thin little girl with large lonely eyes, Annie was a member of a poor, ragged family, traveling in a battered old car, heading west that very day. When Niles tried to learn more about her and the family, he could find no one in Murphy who knew anything about them. He searched volumes of carols and folk tunes. Nowhere could he find the song recorded, and none of the folklorists he knew had heard it before.

The carol, which has become one of a small number of Christmas favorites sung around the world, was published in sheet music by Schirmer Company in 1934.

Here are the lyrics Annie Morgan sang and Niles recorded:

I wonder as I wander out under the sky.
How Jesus the Savior did come for to die
For poor on'ry people like you and like I
I wonder as I wander out under the sky.

When Mary birthed Jesus 'twas in a cow's stall,
With wise men and farmers and shepherds and all.
But high from God's heav'n a star's light did fall
And promise of ages it then did recall.

If Jesus had wanted for any wee thing
A star in the sky or a bird on the wing,
Or all of God's angels in Heaven to sing,
He surely could have it, 'cause He was the King.

Wherever you are Annie Morgan, we hope good fortune and peace will be with you at Christmastime and always for your important gift to the world.

The State, *December 1983*

A Christmas Hymn

by Alfred Domett

It is the calm and silent night!
A thousand bells ring out and throw
Their joyous peal abroad, and smile
The darkness, charmed and holy now!
The night that erst no name had worn,
To it a name is given;
For in that stable lay new-born,
The peaceful Prince of Earth and Heaven,
In the solemn midnight
Centuries ago!

The State, *December 1955*

The Pamlico Holly

by Ruth Peeling in Carteret County News Times

I found it. It wasn't easy, but it's there — the 205-year-old holly tree just across the Craven County line in Pamlico County. It's a gnarled, imposing giant. Not particularly pretty, but would you be pretty at 205 years old?

Lots of folks in these parts didn't know the tree existed until it was publicized in *National Wildlife* magazine in the December 1965 issue. That article was condensed in *Reader's Digest.*

At one time the tree was considered the biggest holly in the United States according to the American Forestry Association's roster of tree giants. But Texas now claims it has a bigger one at Harden in Liberty County.

North Carolina's holly, according to the state forestry division, is 42 inches in diameter above the ground (it looks larger than that; maybe they haven't measured it lately). It is 72 feet high with a crown spread of 45 feet. Because it's a male, it has no berries.

The forestry people say they estimated its age by counting its annual rings, but I don't know how they can count annual rings on the main trunk while the tree is still living and growing.

To reach the tree, follow Route 55 from Bridgeton. About two miles from Bridgeton, there is a paved road that goes to the left. Situated on the left is a white-framed, well-kept church.

Turn on that road, and continue a mile or so until you spot rural mail boxes with the name "Laughinghouse" on the left. About 200 feet beyond those mailboxes is a lane, just two car tracks into a field. The tree is located on the lane, which is in good shape in dry weather.

About 300 feet from the paved road is the tree, enclosed by an anchor chain fence that was erected by the state. The fence can be seen from the paved road if you look closely.

The state forestry division has purchased about four acres of land, which includes the tree. This was accomplished through the effort of the late J.V. Whitfield, a former state senator, and Jackson M. Bachelor of Willard. Bachelor is a former president of the Holly Association of America.

There were no signs directing one to the tree at the time of our visit. There was no plaque of explanation on the fence around it. This may seem strange, but perhaps it is best. People have a terrible impulse to acquire souvenirs, and if the tree were easily accessible, branches and bark might be hacked away, even though it is under protection of the state.

It was a thrill to see the majestic giant, and those who have made an effort to preserve it have done the state and all the people who respect growing things an unusual service.

Effort should be made to protect it from disease. Depending solely on nature's kindness to protect it forever may be expecting too much.

The State, *December 1969*

Merry Christmas, Everyone!

by Maureen Murdocu,
for the Carolina Power & Light Company ad

To little children everywhere —
Reluctant feet upon the stair,
Eyes filled with wonder, ears that hear
Elfin sleighbells drawing near —
Merry, merry Christmas!

To parents who so lovingly
Have decked the star-crowned Christmas Tree,
Then join their neighbors as they go
Caroling across the snow —
Happy, happy Christmas!

To men of good will, far and wide,
Whose hearts and homes this Christmastide
Are opened to the lonely stranger
As their offering to the Manger —
Blessed, blessed Christmas!

The State, *December 1958*

CHAPTER 5

The Santa

Spirit

There's a reason why we cherish the big guy in the red suit. St. Nicholas or Santa Claus, he embodies our dreams, connects us annually to a magical and childlike world, and serves as an ambassador for forgiveness, peace, and love.

Wig and Whiskers

by Bill Stancil

I had been nagged for several years by the question, "What place should Santa Claus have in Christmas?" It seemed that Christ was being pushed aside by commercialism more and more. And now that we had children of our own to rear I wanted to settle my feelings once and for all.

As Christmas of 1968 neared, I asked a local department store Santa Claus if I could take his place for just one hour. He agreed to the idea, so on the appointed night, when the store was full of Christmas shoppers . . . and children waiting for Santa Claus to return to his "throne" in the department store, I donned the red-and-white uniform, the white wig and beard, the black boots, and climbed the magic throne of Santa Claus. What I discovered in the next hour, about children and myself, culminated in my most memorable Christmas.

It's hot behind those snow white whiskers. The chin strap holding the beard fills with sweat in a matter of minutes. The mustache tickles unmercifully, and every now and then I protruded my bottom lip to blow a wisp of the beard out of my mouth. The red-and-white suit did not fit by any stretch of the imagination. The pillow stuffed inside the coat kept trying to slip down into the oversized pants that I was trying my best to hold up. Every time I moved, my body became more damp from the sweat forming inside the suit. The suit was very uncomfortable, and when nobody was looking, I squirmed on my throne to ease the dull ache that enveloped my backside. Finally, a store employee noticed my discomfort and produced an electric fan, which he placed out of sight of the children, directing the oscillating breeze in my direction. I nodded a quiet "thank you" to the salesman and began to ask myself if the experience would be worth the effort.

HO, HO, HO!

The sweat forming inside the suit made me itchy. But before I had a chance to scratch, children were coming up the aisle toward me. "Oh, oh," I thought. "This is it. Wonder how I'll handle the questions?"

A honey-haired, 4-year-old girl cautiously approached me. I did not know which of us was more frightened, but I tried hard not to let my inexperience show.

"Hello there, sweetheart," I said, making my voice as deep and as jolly sounding as I could. Her eyes were all aglow, and I held out my arms to take her upon my knees. She stared at me and smiled ... and something began to happen inside me. The true magic of Christmas had begun to work its way into my soul — although I was not completely aware of it, just yet.

I was prepared for the normal little girl requests — dolls and skates — but I was somewhat taken aback when she hesitated to ask me to bring her a present. "Santa Claus," she said slowly, her soft brown eyes glistening, "do you know what I really want for Christmas?"

At last! We had finally gotten around to what I was hoping she would get around to, and my tension eased some.

"I'd like for you to bring my mommy a towel with her name on it. Her name is Pattie. And you can just pick out something nice for me, and some fruit, if you want to."

Now the real Christmas spirit tightened its grip on me. What an unselfish Christmas request! I choked back the knot in my throat that threatened to burst. I cleared my throat and gave her a squeeze and a piece of candy.

THE DUMP TRUCK

Now the crowd of children, some with parents, grew larger. I silently remind myself not to promise to bring the things they ask for but only to see if it's alright with Mommy and Daddy for children to have the things they ask for.

The children were waiting in line to get upon my lap now and, for a moment, panic seized me. I reached over and pulled a big box of candy nearer my throne so that I could offer each child a candy cane or a sucker. Even though I felt like running, bright little eyes were tearing my feelings to shreds.

"I want a big dump shruck," the sandy-haired, 5-year-old boy said in a manly voice while climbing on my lap. "And I want one this big." He showed me by spreading his arms as far apart as he can.

"Santa Claus," he began again while staring at my beard, "if you can't get a dump shruck, how about a shruck that digs up dirt?"

I started to say something, but he suddenly looked up, rolled his blue eyes, and put his arm around my neck.

"Santa Claus, if I don't get a dump shruck or a shruck that digs in the dirt, then how about any kind of a shruck?"

He also wanted some other things but told me that he could not "member them right now." I handed him a piece of candy, and he took his daddy's hand and waved goodbye.

YOUNG AND WISE

An 8-year-old girl had been standing quietly to one side of my throne, just smiling, for about 15 minutes. She had been inching closer and closer to me as the other children had poured out their Christmas wishes. When she finally decided to climb upon my lap, her conversation belied her age, for it sounded as though it was coming from a much older person.

I had thought that, being 8 years old, the child would see through my fakery. If she did, she didn't let on to me or the other children gathered around my throne.

"I noticed the sign in your seat before you got here," she started right off, as I lifted her to my lap. "The sign said you were out feeding your reindeer."

The sign had been placed on the throne when the regular Santa went to the dressing room to loan me his uniform. So I replied, "Yes. They get very hungry on a long trip."

She quickly told me that her mother was in town to purchase some drapes, and then she snuggled closer to me, placing her arms around my chest. For the first time that evening I began to notice the music on the intercom system, and picked up the strains of "O Little Town of Bethlehem."

"I understand that Rudolph has been sick," she stated matter-of-factly. "When he is sick, does his nose still light up?" I couldn't answer that question right away, so I just nodded my head.

"Maybe he is not getting the right things to eat," she said, diagnosing his problem.

I began to tell myself that perhaps this child wanted to expose my fakery in front of the other children, and I would have been completely at her mercy. If there are story books about Rudolph and sickness, I have not heard of them. She had me! Suddenly, she changed the subject, letting me off the hook. I wiped the sweat from my forehead with a coat sleeve.

Not once had she asked me to bring her anything, so I tried to work the conversation in that direction. She was too quick for me.

"Do you still have that magic island where all of the toys are made?" she wanted to know. "Here we go again," I thought. I had never heard of a magic island. I nodded my head slightly, and she continued her questions.

"Do Dasher and Dancer and the other reindeer like Rudolph better now?" I told her that all of the reindeer get along very well together. "Well, just be sure that Rudolph gets some hot soup to make him feel better in that cold weather."

She did not ask me to bring her anything at all. And her parting concern over Rudolph scored a bull's eye on my heart strings. For a moment, the crowded store and its noisy business transactions became a quiet field of sheep with a few shepherds keeping watch over their flock.

THE SUIT FITS

But the job of being Santa Claus was getting easier, and I could even manage a "Ho-Ho-Ho!" to the youngsters and the adults. The suit seemed to have cooled a bit, and the Christmas carols on the intercom system came through loud and clear over the din of shoppers. People smiled or spoke as they walked by, and I smiled and spoke right back without a moment's hesitation.

My next visitor was about 5 years old, and he really had not made up his mind whether to get near me or not. But urged on by his two sisters, he finally came within reach. He declined the invitation to sit on my lap, preferring to give me his Christmas order with both feet planted firmly on the floor.

"Santa Claus, I want a gutaw for Christmas."

I didn't understand, so I asked him what he said.

"A gutaw," he repeated. "You know . . . a gutaw." This time he made a strumming motion with his hands, and I realized he was trying to say "guitar."

With some bribing with the candy, he told me that he also wanted some trucks, some apples, and some nuts. He had a shopping list for his two sisters, who wanted dolls, and asked me to bring something nice for mommy. He was not sure whether daddy deserved anything or not because "Daddy killed a rabbit yesterday."

I took a few minutes to explain to him that hunting is a sport and that the rabbit would make a fine dinner for him and his family.

After thinking it over for a moment, he came to the conclusion that daddy must be a good shot with a gun and that he would be proud to eat the rabbit. Now it was alright to bring daddy some bedroom shoes and some bullets for his hunting gun.

The Tomboy

A pretty little girl with brown hair cropped short and wearing a toboggan climbed into my lap and stared at me for a minute. Then she gave my beard a quick yank. Fortunately, the chin strap was tied over my head, and the beard did not move. I remembered to yell "Ouch!" and she jumped back. She seemed afraid of me, but her blue eyes were saying "I love you." Since she did not seem to want to talk to me, I started the conversation.

"I'll just bet a pretty little girl like you would love a doll for Christmas," I told her.

"No," her small voice came back. "I want a gun and holster for Christmas." Her father laughed while her mother whispered, "For goodness sakes, you're a daughter, not a son."

Others began to arrive, in ages ranging from a few months to 13 years old. Some of them ran, crying, back to the safety of their parents' arms. For some children it was their first attempt to visit a department store Santa. Others, brave when they left home, were frightened by the time they reached my throne, so I tried to coax them near.

An hour and a half passed, but it seemed like just a few minutes. I wouldn't forget a pair of brown eyes that glistened beneath soft brown hair, for I was especially charmed by the little girl that talked with her eyes and gave Santa a big hug just "for being so nice to me last year."

It was time to "feed the reindeer" again, so I left the throne and walked toward the dressing room, waving goodbye to the children. After changing into my street clothes, I left the store and got into my car. I sat for a few minutes behind the steering wheel, thinking over the events of the past hour and a half. And I again asked myself exactly what place Santa Claus should occupy, if any, in Christmas.

DUTCH UNCLE

Children have a special "hotline" to the North Pole and a rapport with Santa Claus that would put a peace negotiator to envy. And Santa Claus and children have a special corner of life tucked away for their very own that adults may not enter. It's full of desires and wishes that fall only on the ears of the jolly ol' elf.

A child's private world includes a bewhiskered dutch uncle that can solve problems, give advice, and make reindeer fly.

Only Santa Claus understands that "shruck" and "gutaw" are perfectly acceptable words in a child's vocabulary. Only Santa Claus really understands about magic islands, tooth fairies, and hard-working elves.

And who else but Santa Claus would know just how much a little girl wants her mommy to have a towel with her name on it?

Yes, Santa Claus has a proper place in Christmas. He doesn't infringe ... or should not infringe ... on the place Christ occupies in the Christmas Story. Santa Claus is both mythical and real to children. He patiently teaches love, forgiveness, and understanding to children by his own example of giving so freely to children at Christmastime, thus projecting the teachings of Christ.

I sat behind the steering wheel and listened to the music coming from the store: "Hark the Herald Angels Sing," "It Came Upon a Midnight Clear."

The Christmas mystique that exists between children and Santa Claus is mine! I had managed to capture it, at long last, and I realized that I had not just played at being Santa Claus ... for a little while I was Santa Claus.

I turned the ignition switch and whispered quietly, "Giddyap, Rudolph."

The State, *December 1974*

But Which One is the Real Santa?

by Lou Schock Hopchas

Remember how it used to be on the night before
Christmas?

"Tell us about Santa Claus," children would chorus as
they nestled on the laps of their parents.

"Well, once upon a time, long, long ago, before daylight
saving time, Santa Claus came to town but once a year, on
Christmas Eve. He brought toys and goodies for all the little
children, but no one ever saw him, and in fact, the only way
you could get in touch with him was to write him a letter
addressed to the North Pole. That was because Santa was so
busy making toys and getting ready for Christmas, he just
couldn't come before Christmas Eve. But when communications
got better and everyone could finally get in touch with Santa by
dialing direct or using their zip code, they invited him to their
parades so that the children could see him and talk to him in
person. Now, the first Santa Claus would travel around the

world with his sleigh and eight tiny reindeer..."

"But, Daddy, it hardly ever snows here."

"Well, that's why Santa Claus started coming in a helicopter. And now Santa arrives every year on the day after Thanksgiving, and he stays right up until Christmas Eve because there are so many more children than there used to be that it's the only way he can talk to all of them."

"If he stays so long, then who makes all the toys, Daddy?"

"Oh, they're made in factories on mass production lines and then put on television during cartoon shows for all the children to see so that everyone can get exactly what he wants for Christmas. And they're pictured in magazines and toy sections of mail-order catalogs where they are divided into categories, which describe each toy in terms of the learning process. Why, this year, the catalogs say the 6-to-8-year-old boy is approaching Christmas in terms of urban renewal, environmental control, high-rise engineering, and interplanetary communications — batteries not included, of course. This has complicated things awfully for Santa Claus. You see, in the old days, a little girl just wanted a doll. Now, Santa has to remember whether it's a Barbie, Chrissie, Hi Dottie, or Baby Tender Love."

"Wasn't it always like that?"

"Heavens, no! When Santa first came for Christmas there was no such thing as over-choice. He brought simple gifts — apples, oranges, nuts, and little toys made by his elves. There was no such thing as plastic, and everybody was happy with whatever he got. Of course, today's Santa is a little different. He has to be modern. He's part of an affluent society — and he has to keep up. In fact, his real name is Linwood Darris Walker."

"Linwood Darris Walker?" the children exclaimed.

"Why, yes. Every Santa has two names. You know he can't go around in that red suit all the time. So the rest of the time he is Linwood Darris Walker."

"What does he do when he's not wearing his red suit?"

"Oh, he travels a lot — and he thinks about Christmas and children and sends his red suit to the cleaners."

"Where did he come from?"

"He was always here, but one day about three years ago he saw an ad in the paper and was chosen from a selection of several Santa Clauses and became Santa Claus at the shopping center."

"Why can't he be Santa Claus year round?"

"Because we can't have Christmas year round."

"Why?"

"A lot of people have asked that question, but it has never really been answered. It would be a good idea, but it's just never worked out that way."

"Why not?"

"Well because people just forget about Christmas after it's over. The trees and decorations come down. The children have their toys, and mamas and daddies have spent all their money. But the real reason is that the spirit of Christmas gets lost the rest of the year."

"What's the spirit of Christmas, Daddy?"

"Oh, it's love and trust and giving: You see, that's what Christmas is all about, and that's why there is a Santa Claus — to show all the children the spirit of Christmas.

"And if people would be good and kind to each other all the time, why then we could have Christmas all year, and no one would ever notice if Santa Claus were missing."

Linwood Darris Walker, mentioned above, is THE Santa Claus at Tarrytown Shopping Center in Rocky Mount. He is retired from Seaboard Coastline Railroad.

The State, *December 1973*

Where Santa Learned How to Ho-Ho-Ho

by Lewis Philip Hall

Who ever heard of Santa Claus going to school or having his white beard and long hair combed and set in a beauty parlor? Well, our modern Santa in southeastern North Carolina does. The Santa Claus of the 1971 world may also travel in a super sonic jet, in keeping with the age of enlightenment, but his red fur-trimmed suit and cap is the same as it was 149 years ago when Clement C. Moore created it in his immortal "A Visit From St. Nicholas."

Of all the thousands of men that have portrayed Santa Claus across America during the Christmas season, the most famous was the late Charles W. Howard, who for 28 years was Santa Claus at Macy's in New York City. He also rode the float of that company in the mammoth Christmas parade, which is now seen by millions of people on TV.

After retiring in 1937, Mr. Howard, in order to keep

active, conceived the idea of opening a School for Santas, which he did that same year in Albion, New York, 18 miles from Rochester. From that time until his death about nine years ago, Mr. Howard and his able assistant, Nathan Doan of Bay City, Michigan, operated this unique organization. The school still opens on October 15 of each year.

Of the hundreds and hundreds of students that have attended this school from every state in America and also numerous foreign countries, including Australia, there has only been one man that was considered to be a "natural" Santa Claus by the managers, and it is so stated in the school records. That man is Robert Kemp Mills of Wilmington. His career as Santa Claus began around Thanksgiving in 1963, at which time the managers of the Belk-Berry Department Store in Wilmington decided to send Mills to the School for Santas. There he learned how to "Ho-Ho-Ho," how to dance, about the habits of reindeer, how to put on his costume and make-up, how to care for his white beard and shoulder length wig, and to be certain to yell "Ouch!" when it was pulled by an inquisitive child. He also learned the answers to the hundreds of questions that children ask such as, "How are you going to get in my house. I live in a trailer?" The answer: "Santa has a pass key."

A cardinal rule of the school is never promise a child anything. When one asks for a certain kind of toy Santa answers: "I'll see what I can do."

First Professional in N.C.

Mills is a large, tall, handsome man weighing 222 pounds, with a merry twinkle in his blue eyes and a love for children. One knows this by the gentle tender way he cuddles the little fellows in his lap, the concern he has for their every Christmas wish, and the intimate manner he shows for each one.

Seated in his white sleigh, minus the reindeer, surrounded by toys of every description, and dressed in a beautiful red velvet suit and cap trimmed in wide white fur, he's a striking figure. By his side are two large bags, one filled with toys for girls and the other with toys for boys, which he gives to the children of all ages that line up to talk to him.

"The average number that come are about 80 an hour," he said, "but the record for the day is 718."

Twice a week Santa goes to the beauty parlor to have his imported white Yak beard and wig combed and set, and twice a week he also changes his red velvet suit.

Mills is in great demand during the Yuletide season by schools, TV stations, churches, and hospitals in the area.

He has not only the distinction of being the first professional Santa Claus in this state, he is also one of only two in North Carolina, the other being Baxter Butler of Newton.

The School for Santas manager, Nathan Doan, said, "Robert K. Mills is the best and most natural Santa Claus in the history of our school."

What finer compliment could be paid to a man than to say that he is the living, breathing symbol of a character that is loved and adored by all the millions of little ones of this world — the age old Spirit of Christmas.

The State, *December 1971*

A Special Request

by Lucille Noell Dula, Hillsboro

Dear Santa Claus,

Once again, I'm crossing the miles of memory to the years when you were one of the symbols of peace and goodwill throughout the civilized world. In those years Christmas meant Christ, carols, snowflakes feathering down like silver sequins, Santa Claus and his dashing reindeer, and a green tree covered with lights and colored balls, which were no brighter than the shining dreams in the minds and hearts of those who believe in the miracle of Christmas.

In those years, a single toy, plus a stocking filled with assorted nuts, candies, and fruit, could bring a glow in the eyes and faces of children everywhere — a glow reminiscent of that reflected by tall red candles burning on a holly-decked mantle. I want the return of this Christmas glow to the hearts of all people everywhere, so that our own hearts may become lighted altars before the Child of Bethlehem.

Today, Saint Nicholas, I am decorating a tree designed especially to please two boys — one of them whose birthday falls on your night — Christmas Eve.

As I hold each colored ball in my hand, each a symbol of that rosy colored world that I knew as a child, I handle it gently, lest this very symbol of Christmas come to pieces in my hands. As I place each ball on the tree and adjust the colored lights, which still shine through the dark corridors of my mind and heart, I am trying to recapture the wonder of Christmas — but, instead, I hear the roar of guns above the strains of "O Little Town of Bethlehem," and I feel the sharp winds and snows of the battlefields blowing across my thoughts.

A SPECIAL WISH LIST

Tonight, Santa Claus, I am asking for only a few things for Christmas, but in today's world they are so important because we are no longer able to take them for granted. I want the skies of all the world to be filled only with snowflakes and scudding clouds, with one clear star shining out over a midnight world as if to safeguard it from the screams of falling bombs. I want the windows of all the world open — with Christmas lights shining through — and I want Christmas carolers — their coats pulled high against the wind, breaking the frosty silence with their old and young voices — singing in unison.

I want the smell of burning leaves, which reflect in the flames their once crimson and golden hues. I want bountiful harvests resulting in rivers of golden wheat, ruddy winesaps in the bins, golden pumpkins on the shelves, spicy fruit pies, hickory smoked hams, brown-crusted chickens bubbling in the oven — and I want these for all of the hungry and oppressed in every isolated spot and every teeming metropolis throughout this battle-scarred, combat-veteran of a world.

I want a return to the old spirit of giving in which the heart of the giver was bigger than the gift, and Christmas was more than a highly publicized commercial venture. I want this because the Child of Bethlehem — for whom Christmas should be celebrated

— had naught to give but himself, and those who worshipped gave their all from their hearts — not their pigskin wallets.

I want the return of the visions of youth and the dreams of maturity. I want a new belief in the dream that is democracy — a belief that has been lost in an age when men talk largely of power and a gilt-edged kind of security. This nation was not built on power and security but the sweat of honest toil, the pioneer spirit of forging ahead into the unknown, and the banishment of fear and greed because ideals were the predominant stones in the foundation of our nation. The importance of both the individual and his dreams, and the composite dream of a republic, are both facets in the "gem of the ocean," and I want us to recapture the meaning of these two facets of democracy.

I want a return to a peace in which we can concern ourselves with making of democracy a shining symbol, not of plated brass, but of karat gold — a symbol so genuine that from its surface can be reflected the Bill of Rights, the Preamble to the Constitution, and all of the other documents of a free people. It is only such a democracy, Saint Nicholas, that will convince the world that the pot of gold at the end of democracy's rainbow is not the United States Mint.

Finally, Santa Claus, I want a return to the simplicity of everyday living in which we are once more judged by our character and not our wealth, our service and not our notoriety, our generosity and not our extravagance, and our friendliness and not our tolerance, for no one in all the world wishes to be tolerated.

So tonight, Saint Nicholas, let me hear once more your sleigh bells across the crusty snow, let me see your jolly red face flushed on the screen of my memory, and let me feel once more humility before the manger at Bethlehem, joy at the sound of carols, and wonder before my Christmas tree.

For I would feel once again, O kind spirit of unselfishness, the miracle that once was Christmas.

The State, *December 1952*

92